The Best Rock Songs Of All Time

HLE

Hal Leonard Europe
Distributed by Music Sales

Exclusive Distributors:
Music Sales Limited
8/9 Frith Street, London W1V 5TZ, England.
Music Sales Pty Limited
120 Rothschild Avenue, Rosebery, NSW 2018, Australia.

Order No.HLE90000495
ISBN 0-7119-7717-8
This book © Copyright 2000 by Hal Leonard Europe

Cover design by Chloë Alexander
Photographs courtesy of London Features International/Redferns.
Printed in the USA

Your Guarantee of Quality
As publishers, we strive to produce every book to the highest
commercial standards.
The book has been carefully designed to minimise awkward page
turns and to make playing from it a real pleasure.
Throughout, the printing and binding have been planned to
ensure a sturdy, attractive publication which should give years
of enjoyment.
If your copy fails to meet our high standards, please inform us
and we will gladly replace it.

Music Sales' complete catalogue describes thousands of titles
and is available in full colour sections by subject, direct from
Music Sales Limited. Please state your areas of interest and send
a cheque/postal order for £1.50 for postage to:
Music Sales Limited, Newmarket Road, Bury St. Edmunds,
Suffolk IP33 3YB, England.

www.internetmusicshop.com

ADDICTED TO LOVE

Words and Music by
ROBERT PALMER

9

AFRICA

Words and Music by DAVID PAICH
and JEFF PORCARO

3° To Coda ⊕

I bless the rains____ down in Af - - - ri - ca,____

gon - na take some time to do____ the things we nev - er had.____

D.%. al Coda

Verse 2:
The wild dogs cry out in the night
As they grow restless longing for some solitary company.
I know that I must do what's right
Sure as Kilimanjaro rises like an empress above the Serengeti.
I seek to cure what's deep inside
Frightened of this thing that I've become.

Verse 3:
Instrumental
Pretty boy she's waiting there for you.

ALL RIGHT NOW

Words and Music by PAUL RODGERS
and ANDY FRASER

ALL ALONG THE WATCHTOWER

Words and Music by
BOB DYLAN

ALL SHOOK UP

Words and Music by OTIS BLACKWELL
and ELVIS PRESLEY

hands are sha - ky and my knees are weak. _ I can't seem to stand _ on my

own two feet, _ Who do you thank when you have such luck? _ I'm in

Eb7   F7

love! I'm all shook up! _ Mm _ mm oh, oh, yeah, _

Bb Eb7 Bb   Eb7

yeah! _____

1. Please don't ask what's _ on my mind, _ I'm a
2. Tongue gets tied when I try to speak, _ My _

ALWAYS

Words and Music by
JON BON JOVI

31

32

Well, there ain't no luck ___ in these

BORN TO BE WILD

Words and Music by
MARS BONFIRE

Get your mo-tor run - ning. Head out on the high - way
I like smoke and light - ning, heav - y met - al thun - der

look - ing for ad - ven - ture in what
rac - ing in the wind and the

ev - er comes our way. Yeah, dar - ling, gon - na
feel - ing that I'm un - der.

BACK IN THE U.S.S.R.

Words and Music by JOHN LENNON
and PAUL McCARTNEY

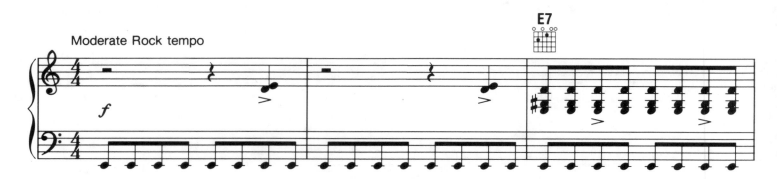

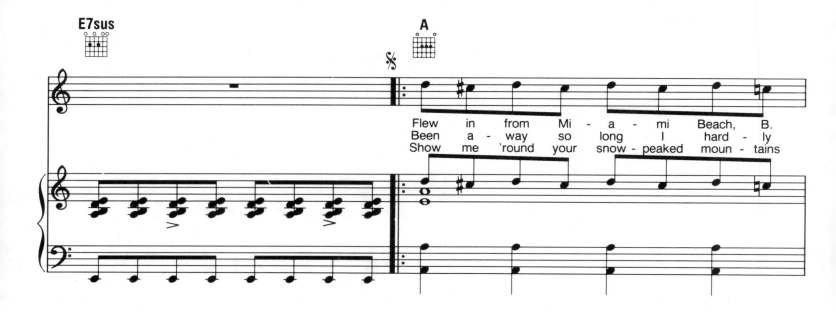

Flew in from Mi - a - mi Beach, B.
Been a - way so long I hard - ly
Show me 'round your snow - peaked moun - tains

O. A. C., Did - n't get to bed last night. On
knew the place, Gee it's good to get back home. Leave
way down south, Take me to your dad - dy's farm. Let

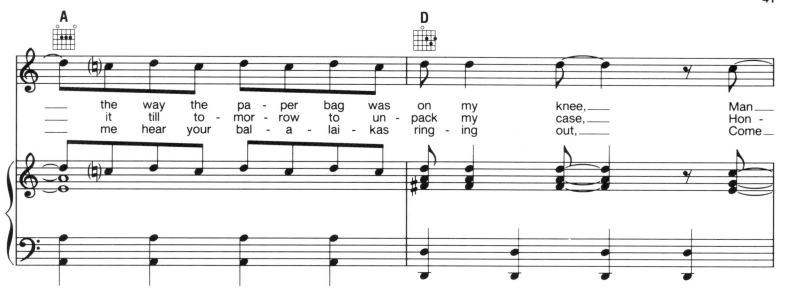

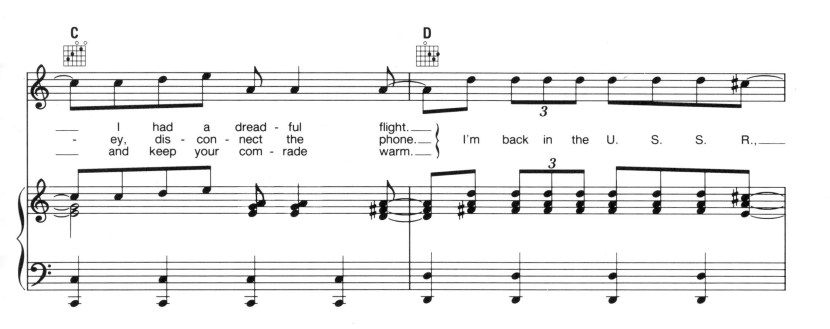

BAND ON THE RUN

Words and Music by
McCARTNEY

Brighter beat

1. Well, the

rain ex - plod - ed with a might - y crash__ As we fell in - to__ the sun,__
un - der - tak - er drew a heav - y sigh__ See - ing no one else__ had come,__
night was fall - ing as the des - ert world__ Be - gan to set - tle down.__

And the first one said to the sec - ond one there__ I hope you're hav - ing fun.__
And a bell was ring - ing in the vil - lage square For the rab - bits on the run.__
In the town they're search - ing for us ev - 'ry where__ But we nev - er will be found.__

Band on the run,___ Band on the run;___ 1.2. And the
3. And the

jail - er man___ and sail - or Sam___ Were search - ing ev - 'ry one ⎫ For the
coun - ty judge___ who held a grudge___ Will search for ev - er more ⎬

Band on__the run,___ Band on__the run,___ Band on__the run,___

1.2. Band on__the run.___ 2. Well, the 3. Band on__the run.___
3. Well, the

BROTHERS IN ARMS

Words and Music by
MARK KNOPFLER

(Guitar solo)

There's so ma-ny diffe-rent worlds.   so ma-ny diffe-rent

suns   and we have just one   world

but we live in diffe-rent ones.

Guitar solo

Now the sun's gone to hell ___

CROCODILE ROCK

Words and Music by ELTON JOHN
and BERNIE TAUPIN

Light-hearted Rock

56

But the years___   I re - mem -

A DESIGN FOR LIFE

Music by JAMES DEAN BRADFIELD and SEAN MOORE
Lyrics by NICKY WIRE

62

Verses 2:
I wish I had a bottle
Right here in my dirty face,
To wear the scars
To show from where I came.

Verses 3:
I wish I had a bottle
Right here in my pretty face,
To wear the scars
To show from where I came.

DON'T LOOK BACK IN ANGER

Words and Music by
NOEL GALLAGHER

1. Slip in-side___ the eye of your mind,_____ don't you know you might___ find___
(Verse 2 see block lyric)

a bet-ter place to play._____

Verse 2:
Take me to the place where you go
Where nobody knows if it's night or day
Please don't put your life in the hands
Of a rock 'n' roll band who'll throw it all away.

I'm gonna start a revolution from my head
'Cause you said the brains I had went to my head
Step outside, the summertime's in bloom
Stand up beside the fireplace, take that look from off your face
'Cause you ain't never gonna burn my heart out.

DON'T SPEAK

Words and Music by ERIC STEFANI
and GWEN STEFANI

70

DON'T LOSE MY NUMBER

Words and Music by
PHIL COLLINS

EVERY BREATH YOU TAKE

Words and Music by
STING

FIELDS OF GOLD

Written and Composed by
STING

Flowing, moderately

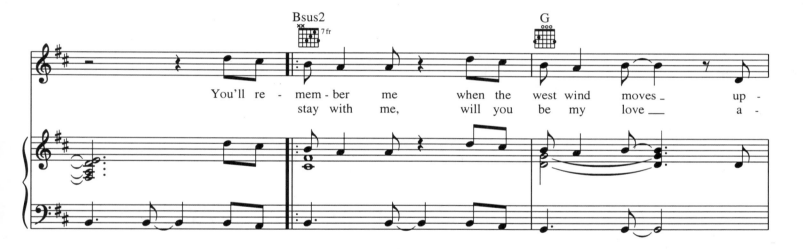

You'll re-mem-ber me, when the west wind moves _ up a-
stay with me, when will you be my love _ a-

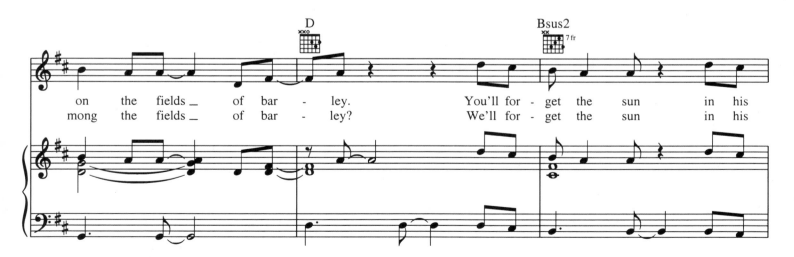

on the fields _ of bar - ley. You'll for - get the sun in his
mong the fields _ of bar - ley? We'll for - get the sun in his

GET BACK

Words and Music by JOHN LENNON
and PAUL McCARTNEY

Jo Jo was a man who thought he was a lon-er, But
Instrumental
Sweet Lor-et-ta Mar-tin thought she was a wom-an, But
Instrumental

___ he knew it could-n't last. ___
___ she was an-oth-er man. ___
Jo ___ Jo left his home in Tuc-
All ___ the girls a-round her say

-son Ar-i-zo-na, for ___ some Cal-i-for-nia grass. }
___ she's got it com-ing, But ___ she gets it while she can. ___

Get back! ___

GOOD VIBRATIONS

Words and Music by BRIAN WILSON and MIKE LOVE
Music by BRIAN WILSON

94

GOODBYE YELLOW BRICK ROAD

Words and Music ELTON JOHN
and TAUPIN

Moderately slow, in 2

When are you gon-na come down   When are   you going   to land_
What do you think you'll   do then   I bet that-'ll shoot down_____   your plane_

_____   I should have stayed _ on the farm _   Should have list -ened_ to my_____ old man_
_____   It-'ll take you a cou -ple of vod -ka and ton -ics to   set you on your feet a-gain_

_____   You know you can't hold _ me for-ev-er_____   I did-n't sign up_ with you_____
_____   May-be you'll get_____ a re-place -ment   there's plen-ty like   me to be found_

GREAT BALLS OF FIRE

Words and Music by OTIS BLACKWELL
and JACK HAMMER

A HARD DAY'S NIGHT

Words and Music by JOHN LENNON
and PAUL McCARTNEY

HARD TO SAY I'M SORRY

Words and Music by PETER CETERA
and DAVID FOSTER

I CAN SEE FOR MILES

Words and Music by
PETER TOWNSHEND

Bright Rock

I know you've de- ceived me. Now here's a sur- prise.

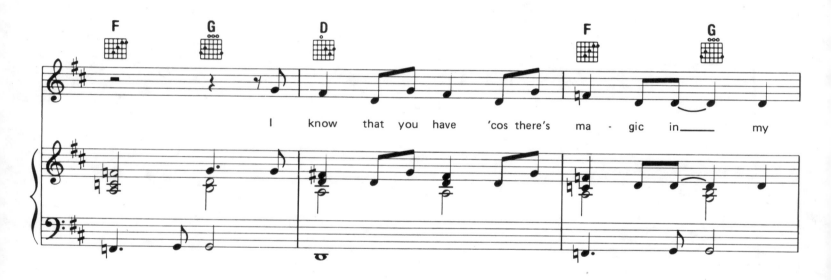

I know that you have 'cos there's ma- gic in_____ my

eyes.   I can see for miles and   miles and

I JUST WANT TO MAKE LOVE TO YOU

By WILLIE DIXON

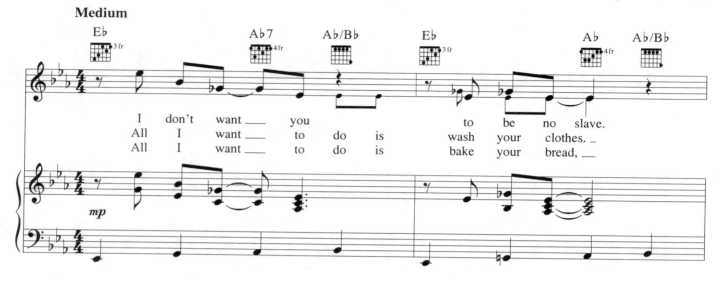

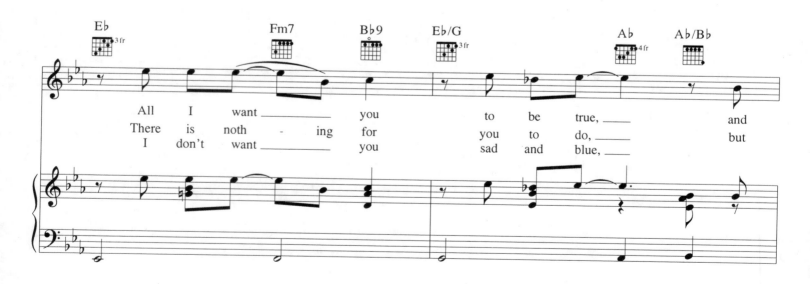

I SAW HER STANDING THERE

Words and Music by JOHN LENNON
and PAUL McCARTNEY

Well, she was just sev - en - teen, and you and I,
looked at me and you and I,

know what I mean, I could see
I could see And the way she looked was way
That be - fore too long I'd

fall be - yond com - pare. her.
in love with So

I STILL HAVEN'T FOUND WHAT
I'M LOOKING FOR

Words by BONO
Music by U2

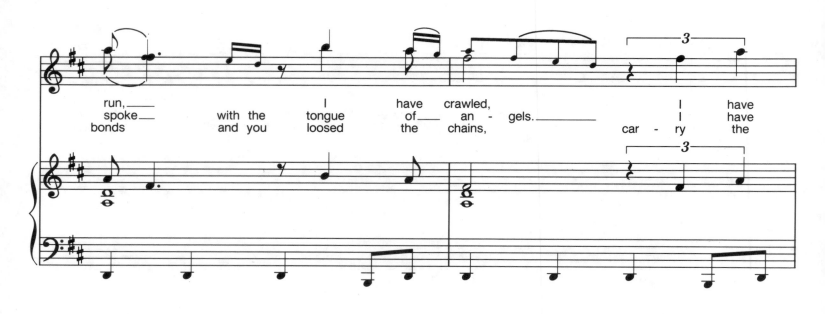

run,_____ I have crawled, I have
spoke_____ with the tongue of_____ an - gels._____

bonds and you loosed the chains, car - ry have the

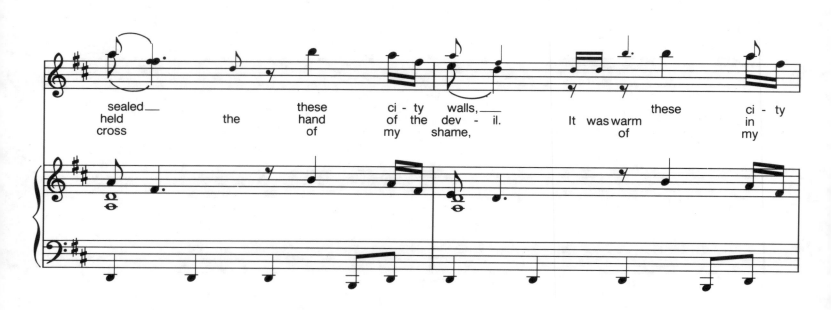

sealed_____ these ci - ty walls,_____ these ci - ty
held the these hand of the dev - il. It was warm
cross of my shame, of in my

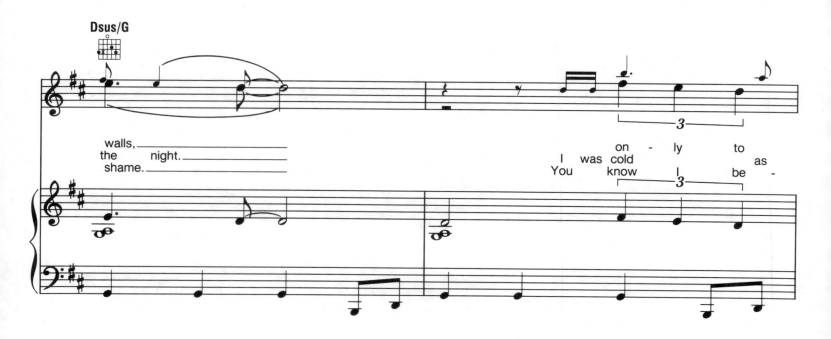

Dsus/G

walls,_____
the night._____ on - ly to
shame._____ I was cold as
You know I be -

ing for. _____ I have

IF YOU LOVE SOMEBODY SET THEM FREE

Words and Music by
STING

I WANT TO KNOW WHAT LOVE IS

Words and Music by
MICK JONES

I bet-ter read be-tween the lines,___ in case I need it when_ I'm old - er.___

Now, this moun-tain I_ must climb___ feels like the world up-on___ my shoul-
I'm gon-na take a lit-tle time,___ a lit-tle time to look_ a-round___

change this lone - ly life._____ I want to know what love_ is.___

I want you to show_ me.

I want to feel what love_is.___ I know you can show_ me.___

D.S. and fade

__ me.

IMAGINE

Words and Music by
JOHN LENNON

142

LAYLA

Words and Music by ERIC CLAPTON
and JIM GORDON

What will you do when you get lone - ly
Tried to give you con - so - la - tion,
Let's make the best of the sit - u - a - tion

JOHNNY B. GOODE

Words and Music by
CHUCK BERRY

LIGHT MY FIRE

Words and Music by
THE DOORS

LOUIE, LOUIE

Words and Music by
RICHARD BERRY

LIKE A ROLLING STONE

Words and Music by
BOB DYLAN

Verse 2. You've gone to the finest school all right Miss Lonely,
But you know you only used to get
Juiced in it.
And nobody's ever taught you how to live on the street
And now you're gonna have to get
Used to it.
You said you'd never compromise
With the mystery tramp, but now you realize
He's not selling any alibis
As you stare into the vacuum of his eyes
And ask him do you want to
Make a deal?

Refrain:

Verse 3. You never turned around to see the frowns on the jugglers and the clowns
When they all come down
And did tricks for you
You never understood that it ain't no good
You shouldn't let other people
Get your kicks for you.
You used to ride on the chrome horse with your diplomat
Who carried on his shoulder a Siamese cat,
Ain't it hard when you discovered that
He really wasn't where it's at
After he took from you everything
He could steal.

Refrain:

Verse 4. Princess on the steeple
And all the pretty people're drinkin', thinkin'
That they got it made.
Exchanging all kinds of precious gifts and things
But you'd better lift your diamond ring,
You'd better pawn it babe,
You used to be so amused
At Napoleon in rags and the language that he used
Go to him now, he calls you, you can't refuse
When you got nothing, you got nothing to lose,
You're invisible now, you got no secrets
To conceal.

Refrain:

LIVIN' ON A PRAYER

Words and Music by JON BON JOVI,
RICHIE SAMBORA and DESMOND CHILD

Liv - in' on ___ a prayer. ___

(Instrumental)

Oh, _____ we've got to

MAYBE I'M AMAZED

Words and Music by
PAUL McCARTNEY

1. Ba-by I'm a-mazed at the way you
3. May-be I'm a-mazed at the way you're
2-4: *Instrumental ad lib solo*

love me all the time,__ And may-be I'm a-fraid of the way I
with me all the time,__ And may-be I'm a-fraid of the way I

love you.__ May-be I'm a-mazed at the way you
need you.__ May-be I'm a-mazed at the way you

MISS YOU

Words and Music by ERIC CLAPTON,
GREG PHILLINGANES and BOBBY COLUMBY

170

MORE THAN A FEELING

Words and Music by
TOM SCHOLZ

Medium Rock

I woke up this morn - ing and the sun was gone. I
So man - y peo - ple have come and gone; the

turned up the mu - sic to start my day. I
fac - es fade as the years go by, yet

When I'm tired____ and think-ing cold,   I hide in my mu - sic, for-

NIGHTS IN WHITE SATIN

Words and Music by
JUSTIN HAYWARD

180

NO SON OF MINE

Words and Music by TONY BANKS,
PHIL COLLINS and MIKE RUTHERFORD

1. Well the

key to my ___ sur - vi - val was ne - ver in much doubt, ___
See block lyrics for Verses 2&3

184

Oh his words how__ they hurt me, I'll ne-ver for-get it,

and as the time it__ went by,__ I lived to re-gret

it. You're no son,__ you're no son__ of mine.__ But where should I go,__

__ and what should I do?__ You're no son,__ you're no son__ of mine.__

Verse 2:
I didn't think much about it
'Til it started happening all the time.
Soon I was living with the fear every day
Of what might happen that night.
I couldn't stand to hear the crying
Of my mother, and I remember when
I swore that, that would be the last they'd see of me,
And I never went home again.

Verse 3: (D.S.)
Well the years passed so slowly,
I thought about him everyday,
What would I do if we passed on the street,
Would I keep running away?
In and out of hiding places,
Soon I'd have to face the facts,
That we'd have to sit down and talk it over,
And that would mean going back.

REELIN' IN THE YEARS

Words and Music by WALTER BECKER
and DONALD FAGEN

MCA Music Publishing

PRIDE
(In the Name of Love)

Words by BONO
Music by U2

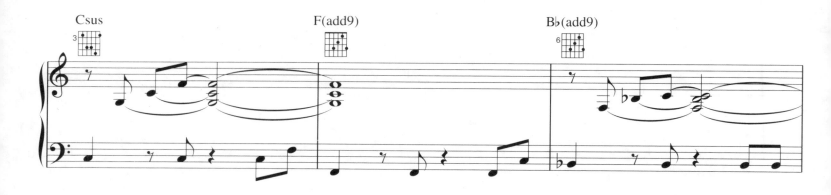

RHYTHM OF THE NIGHT

Words and Music by
DIANE WARREN

(1.) I know a place where we can dance the whole night a-way   un-der-neath e-lec-tric
(2.,3.) come join the fun, this ain't no time to be stay-ing home,   ooh, there's too much go-ing

stars.   Just come with me and we can shake your blues right a-way.
on.   To-night is gon-na be a night like you've nev-er known;

To Coda

You'll be do-ing fine once the mu-sic starts,   oh.
We're gon-na have a good time the whole night long,   oh.   Feel the beat of the rhy-thm of __ the

night, dance un-til the morn - ing light. For-get a-bout the wor-ries on__ your

RIKKI DON'T LOSE THAT NUMBER

Words and Music by WALTER BECKER
and DONALD FAGEN

ROCKET MAN
(I Think It's Gonna Be a Long Long Time)

Words and Music by ELTON JOHN
and BERNIE TAUPIN

Moderately slow, with a beat

ROXANNE

Words and Music by
STING

SCHOOL'S OUT

Words and Music by ALICE COOPER, NEAL SMITH,
MICHAEL BRUCE, GLEN BUXTON and DENNIS DUNAWAY

216

SIMPLY THE BEST

Words and Music by MIKE CHAPMAN
and HOLLY KNIGHT

Moderate rock

(1.) I call you, I need you, my heart's on fire.
(Verses 2 & 3 see block lyric)

You come to me, come to me,

walk-ing a - way__ with my heart__ and my soul.__

I can feel your rhy-thm

when I'm a - lone.__

Oh ba - by, you're my soul.__

You're the best__

VERSE 2:
Give me a lifetime of promises, and a world of dreams
Speak the language of love like you know what it means
Mm, and it can't be wrong
Take my heart and make it strong babe.

VERSE 3:
In your heart, in the stars, every night and every day
In your eyes I get lost, I get washed away
Just as long as I'm here in your arms
I could be in no better place.

STAYIN' ALIVE

Words and Music by BARRY GIBB,
MAURICE GIBB and ROBIN GIBB

Medium Rock beat

Well, you can tell

___ by the way I use___ my walk,___ I'm a wom-an's man; no time to talk.___
___ get___ low and I___ get high,___ and if I___ can't get ei-ther, I real-ly try.___ Got the

Mu-sic loud___ and wom-en warm,___ I've been kicked a-round___ since I___ was born. And now it's
wings of heav-en on___ my shoes.___ I'm a danc-in' man___ and I just can't lose.___ You know it's

226

SULTANS OF SWING

Words and Music by
MARK KNOPFLER

Additional Verses

3. You check out Guitar George, he knows all the chords.
   Mind he's strictly rhythm, he doesn't want to make it cry or sing.
   An old guitar is all he can afford,
      when he gets up under the lights, to play his thing.

4. And Harry doesn't mind if he doesn't make the scene.
   He's got a daytime job and he's doin' all right.
   He can play honky-tonk just like anything,
      savin' it up for Friday night
      with the Sultans, with the Sultans of swing.

5. And a crowd of young boys, they're foolin' around in the corner,
      drunk and dressed in their best brown baggies and their platform soles.
   They don't give a damn about any trumpet playin' band;
      it ain't what they call rock and roll.
   And the Sultans of swing played Creole.

6. *Instrumental*

7. And then The Man, he steps right up to the microphone
      and says, at last, just as the time-bell rings:
   "Thank you, good night, now it's time to go home."
   And he make it fast with one more thing:
   "We are the Sultans of Swing."

   (To Coda)

SURFIN' U.S.A.

Lyrics by BRIAN WILSON
Music by CHUCK BERRY

Solid shuffle beat

If ev-'ry-bod-y had an o - cean a-cross the U. S. A.,
(We'll all be plan-nin' out a) route we're gon-na take real soon

Then ev-'ry-bod-y'd be surf - in' like Cal-i-for-ni - a.
We're wax-in' down our surf - boards we can't wait for June.

You'd see them wear-in' their bag - gies, huar-a-chi san-dals too.
We'll all be gone for the sum - mer, we're on sa-fa-ri to stay.

A bush-y bush-y blonde hair - do, Surf-in' U. S. A.
Tell the teach-er we're surf - in, Surf-in' U. S. A.

WILD WOOD

Words and Music by
PAUL WELLER

try - ing, you're gon - na find your way out of the

wild, wild wood. Said you're gon - na find your way out

of the wild, wild _ wood. ____

1.

Of the

2.

Verse 2:
Don't let them get you down,
Making you feel guilty about
Golden rain will bring you riches,
All the good things you deserve now.

Verse 3:
Climbing, forever trying,
Find your way out of the wild wild wood.
Now there's no justice,
You've only yourself that you can trust in.

Verse 4:
And I said high tide, mid-afternoon,
People fly by in the traffic's boom.
Knowing just where you're blowing,
Getting to where you should be going.

Verse 5:
Day by day your world fades away,
Waiting to feel all the dreams that say,
Golden rain will bring you riches,
All the good things you deserve now.

WON'T GET FOOLED AGAIN

Words and Music by
PETE TOWNSHEND

ZOMBIE

Lyrics and Music by
DOLORES O'RIORDAN

An-oth-er head hangs low-ly, child _ is slow-ly tak-
An-oth-er moth-er's break-in' heart _ is tak-ing o-

en.
ver.
And the vi-'lence caused _ such si-lence, who _
When the vi-'lence caus-es si-lence, we _

YOU REALLY GOT ME

Words and Music by
RAY DAVIES

247